P9-ARK-901

Helicopters

Kate Riggs

CREATIVE EDUCATION • CREATIVE PAPERBACKS

seedlings

Published by Creative Education and Creative Paperbacks
P.O. Box 227, Mankato, Minnesota 56002
Creative Education and Creative Paperbacks
are imprints of The Creative Company
www.thecreativecompany.us

Design by Ellen Huber
Production by Travis Green
Art direction by Rita Marshall
Printed in Malaysia

Photographs by Alamy (Accent Alaska.com, Air Collection,
Ashley Cooper, Ashley Cooper pics), Dreamstime (Ken Backer,
Luis Fernando Chavier, Dani3315, Elena Elisseeva, Charlotte
Erpenbeck, Anthony Hathaway, Charles Mccarthy, Monkey
Business Images, Navarone, Francesca Perticucci, Paul
Prescott, Speedfighter17, Swinnerrr, Dan Van Den Broeke),
iStockphotos (Farm66)

Library of Congress Cataloging-in-Publication Data
Riggs, Kate.
Helicopters / Kate Riggs.
p. cm. — (Seedlings)
Includes bibliographical references and index.
Summary: A kindergarten-level introduction to helicopters,
covering their pilots, equipment, role in rescuing, and such
defining features as their rotors.
ISBN 978-1-60818-582-5 (hardcover)
ISBN 978-1-62832-187-6 (pbk)
1. Helicopters—Juvenile literature. I. Title.

TL716.2.R54 2015
629.133'352—dc23   2014034720

CCSS: RI.K.1, 2, 3, 4, 5, 6, 7;
RI.1.1, 2, 3, 4, 5, 6, 7; RF.K.1, 3; RF.1.1

First Edition HC 9 8 7 6 5 4 3 2 1
First Edition PBK 9 8 7 6 5 4 3 2 1

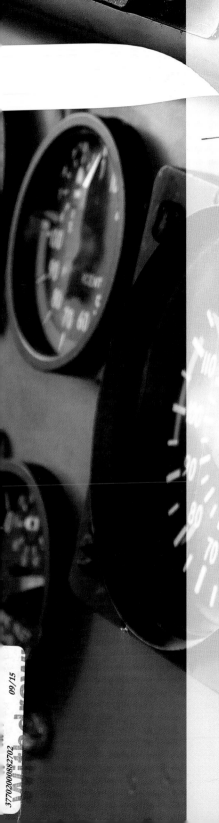

TABLE OF CONTENTS

Time
to help!

Helicopters help people who

are lost.

They take care
of hurt people.

Helicopters fly like airplanes. But they use rotors to move up and down. They can go sideways, too.

A helicopter can land almost anywhere.

It has wheels or
parts called skids
to help it land.

Two people fly the helicopter.
They sit in the front.

Other workers
sit behind them.

A worker uses a strong
cable to lift someone into
the cab.

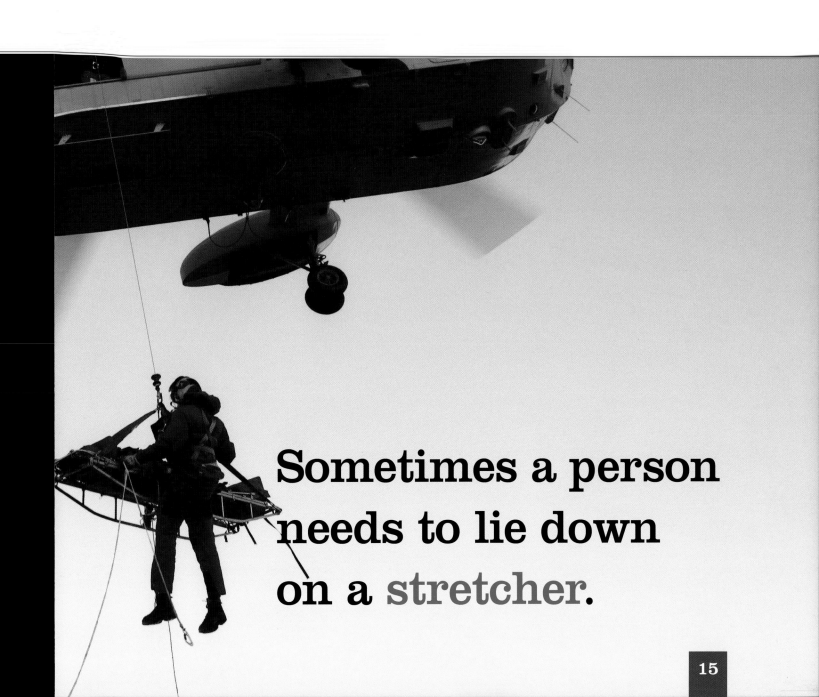

Sometimes a person needs to lie down on a stretcher.

The helicopter flies to the hospital. Then it goes back to its base.

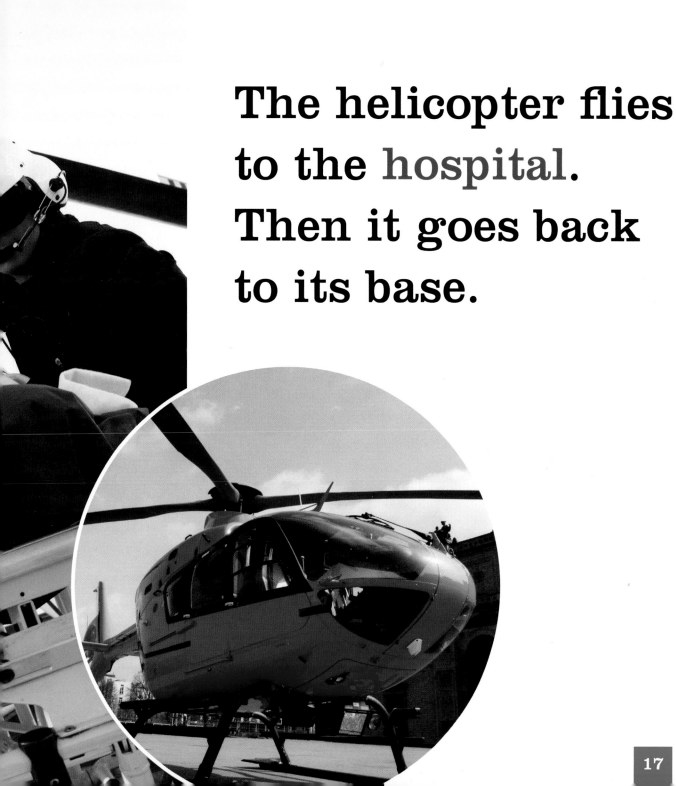

Ready to help again!

Picture a Helicopter

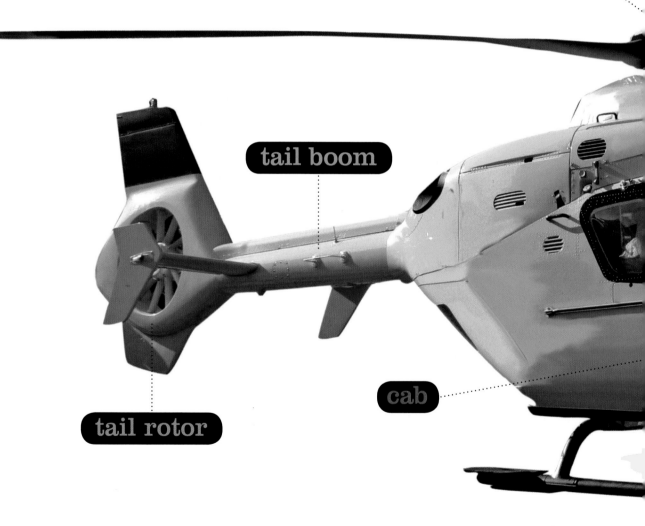

main rotor

tail boom

tail rotor

cab

blades

cockpit

skids

Words to Know

cab: the part of the helicopter that holds people

hospital: the place where doctors and nurses work to help people heal

rotors: parts of a helicopter that move around to lift the vehicle in the air

stretcher: a special bed on wheels used in an ambulance or helicopter

Read More

Chancellor, Deborah. *Police Rescue*.
Mankato, Minn.: Smart Apple Media, 2014.

Lindeen, Mary. *Helicopters*.
Minneapolis: Bellwether Media, 2008.

Websites

Helicopter Dot-to-Dot
http://www.first-school.ws/t/ap/helicopter_dot_to_dot10.htm
Do this dot-to-dot to make a helicopter, then color
your picture.

Rescue Zone Puzzles
http://www.airrescue.co.nz/Kids-Activity-Page/Puzzles
/puzzles-spot-difference-maze-__I.11364
Play air rescue games, and take a safety quiz.

Index